She Calls in the Dead of Night

She Calls in the Dead of Night

DAWN IN THE DARK

Joseph Michael Shucraft

RESOURCE *Publications* • Eugene, Oregon

SHE CALLS IN THE DEAD OF NIGHT
Dawn in the Dark

Copyright © 2025 Joseph Michael Shucraft. All rights reserved. Except for brief quotations in critical publications or reviews, no part of this book may be reproduced in any manner without prior written permission from the publisher. Write: Permissions, Wipf and Stock Publishers, 199 W. 8th Ave., Suite 3, Eugene, OR 97401.

Resource Publications
An Imprint of Wipf and Stock Publishers
199 W. 8th Ave., Suite 3
Eugene, OR 97401

www.wipfandstock.com

PAPERBACK ISBN: 979-8-3852-3985-6
HARDCOVER ISBN: 979-8-3852-3986-3
EBOOK ISBN: 979-8-3852-3987-0

02/24/25

In hopes of better times and better seasons.
For a better way of living and good promises for my future.

CONTENTS

Introduction — xi

Part I

Awakening from Death's Deceit — 3
    Numb — 4
    Song in the Dark — 5
    Attraction in the Dawn — 6

By Night's Early Light — 7
    Light in My Frozen Heart — 8
    Never To Love Without You — 9
    Pleading for your Prayers — 11

Slumbering Wake — 12
    Past Time to Dig — 13
    From the Grave to the Garden — 14
    Waking in The Dark — 15

Prevailing Winds — 16
    Lift Me Up — 17
    Like A Wildfire — 18
    Standing Tall — 19

Desert Lands — 20
    Grains of Sand — 21
    Serpents Defeat — 22
    Parched in the Heat — 23

Interlude — 24

Part II

All in Time	27
There She Stands	28
Boldness of the Prince	29
Who am I?	30
The Breaking Wind	31
Soaring Eagles	32
Warmer Waters	33
Home and Hearth	34
Passing the Idle Time	35
Picking up the Pieces	36
Without Him	37
Waking up to Her	38
Darling in the Evening	39
In Your Greatest Measure	40
The Grace that Breaks	41
Waiting for You	42
Soldier of Fortune	43
On the Plains of Heaven	44
Fighting the Past	45
Come Lord Jesus Come	46
Bless Us, O Lord	47
Sanctify Our Spirits	48
Justify Our Steps	49
Interlude	50

Seeking the Lost Way	51
Whether Near or Far	52
Death's Shadow	53
Fires of Virtue	55
Words of Wisdom	57
The Ruler	58
The Foolish Man	59
The Sightless Beggar	60
Author's Thoughts	61
John 3:1–21 (KJV)	63

INTRODUCTION

When I met you, I was hurting and in pain—waking up feeling saner. I had no reason to believe it. But when I talked to you, I felt anew. There was something to make me hopeful. I could count on ears to hear. I broke free from my madness. I am furthering my cause to build upon this mountain a specific pillar that stands in the triumph of where I have been. The beautiful scenery was yours and mine when we gathered. I am thankful for all I got and have gotten. But I cannot help but be reminded of where I have been inwardly . . .

PART I

AWAKENING FROM DEATH'S DECEIT

One day, I became numb and callous. Deceit entered my temperament, a cruel disregard for my emotional turmoil—burdening and burgeoning suffering abandoning me incomplete and barren. A dark precipice hallowed out, droll an endless tirade. Voices competing thoughts will retreating into a hallway of horror and despair. The agony of my mind, the invested ghost, is replete—like a wading swallow drowning in a blood-red sea. This beam of vested ruse hits me with the demon's eyes—no path to but a dead-end vice. Thrice, I waded into the cavern. Ten times, if I constantly dreamed, I would wake. Will you ever take a breath or lie down without peace and sanity? Please recover me from this persistent warfare of intellect. The transformation of insecurity increases my diligence and resurrects my soul. The exquisiteness in view shatters the mold and returns my heart to a rejuvenated condition. A person of object and a gem of the spirit, gather and hold me arm in arm.

Numb

Demise to end, my age of decay.
A shallow man's tomb, a constant day's façade
Will I break in the day?
I am dying in the quiet of the night.
Flicker the shutters and fasten the windows.
It was concealed from the circle of pain and torment.
Death's kiss is no bliss, I reminisce.
The cold crept in one day, and I bore all.
Why not disappear from an Earth filled with lies?
Why not run when tears are held dry, and humanity passes?
My eyes are collapsed, and the dirt is laid.
Embers from ash to eat dust and cradled sepulcher.
Weep and become weary.
Stuck in the past, I lay dreary.
Please save me.
I am praying for the breaking of the day.

Song in the Dark

Lurking in the shadows, the darkest corners of my mind
A banished sentiment long hastened by the coldness of the draft.
A tempered rift in the wind said, "You are riddled with sin."
Turn me over and banish me to the outer rifts.
Entwine me in misery, a shattered and ragged memory.
There is no cause for these harrowing, deep-rooted shackles.
Remain seeking love to bring me from this sleep.
A melody in the dark sounds so sweet.
Begging me to join in and dance by chance.
Please search for a way to fill the way I dream.
Of a garden of blossoms, which showcases our lovely embrace.
Advent by daylight, a profound winter chill
End of the flora bringing an end to my love
Harmonious rhapsody, the alteration of my mind
The way, the air, the heart I need.

Attraction in the Dawn

A harmonious soliloquy, a keepsake of reminiscence
Wondering why, with a wounded eye, the transition from the dark
To a sunrise filled with a radiant smile and gleaming eyes
Upon the lakeside meadow stands my prize
Tattered rags stand in hand and pour into me a reprimand.
Why or why not peer within?
Set aside my defiant nature.
Settle down in the morning.
She makes a man quake till daybreak, and the timid grow bold.
In the silence between our moments, we were growing apart.
This paradise of harmony, a flowing river cultivated.
This day, our time, I hope, shall never pass by
Never Idle nor weary blind not dreary
Seeing you in my mind

BY NIGHT'S EARLY LIGHT

Relegated to a task and unable to hold on. Offbeat and unsure, a gorge settled amongst two hills. Where two meet, one ends another a valley, the other bends. Trying for a route, a direction with no triumph but rather destitution. Oh, by the wayside, goes this man down into the earliest of the nights. Where the darkness lingers, and highest among them is me, cavorted like an entertainer with no gathering. The duality of thought is fragmented into despair and reason. Logic says I should chase the pleasant maiden till the break of day, and what a finer life with happiness and a wife may be. My brain is torn, split, ripped apart by insanity. Beg me a pardon, for I will shed my honor and leave a kind word, which I seek, worn down though I am bleak. Chasing my sanity sounds rather insane since it is twice lost and beaten in vain. Examine me and take, pray for me, and speak? There is no way for me to close this mountainous sin. So, I implore you to plead for both you and for me. Will you love me like the father? Set me aside, kick dirt, and bury me as I die? Will I meet her in the end on the trail wind in the setting of the sunshine until the early rising of the sun?

Light in My Frozen Heart

She is wearing black, and it is a wedding day funeral.
Masquerading as a present-day miracle
Down by the stream where you and I rest and reside.
It was the shining light toiling at night.
She rode in the dark and swore allegiance to light.
An intensity in her eyes within me would ignite.
A love sparing the dread of my tainted life.
In me was borne the ice, wind, and fire.
Sitting in front of a winter starlit bonfire
Eyes meeting eyes and the flickering of the soul
I am running with only half of my heart.
The other left behind with her shattered in the dark

Never To Love Without You

Passing by my hopes were instilled.
No less a girl as sweet as thee
A chance, a place I pray you to be.
Will you be the only one who is stunning to me?
Best of friends and quietest of banters
Elegant one of extravagance
Camaraderie is all I seek when I gaze upon this pleasant stream.
Where is this time or space?
To be lost, stranded in the daze of a dream, asleep.
I would wake up to a glint like a disguise.
Never to blink but rapture in delight
I run, hide, panic, fleeing my mind.
Where did it go the glory of her grace?
What stood face-to-face again?
A seeing of the eyes and all breadth apace
Will I cry till bloodshed and die?
I am waking and listening to the voice of reason.
A sense of calling out to me
Tireless, never-ceasing disharmony.
Am I crazed or simply in agony?
From where I stand to where I will go
A place, apace, and the evaporated flow.
Endless legacy of beauty.
With starlit eyes and hair full and quaint
Voluptuous and sanctimonious the labor of my heart
She is by likelihood to be the loveliest of 10,000 and 10,000 more.

I would part with my arm for only one goodbye.

Today, my inheritance will be a final call, one remaining declaration.

A moment, a chance, one last glance

Another time to seek and speak.

To love and not lose but instead enjoy and cherish.

In your memory, I strive.

To hold this cheerfulness

Pleading for your Prayers

I am passing away inside from a state of brainwashing.
The rearranging of my life leads me down a side road.
Passageways and curtains the exit from this scene.
Please talk to me, breathe into my life
Hearing her calling, she says, "I'll pray for rain tonight."
To water your insides to grow your mind and give you peace today.
Shouting out glory for me and you. I will see you, and I will speak.
My hope for you and me is to dance together in that rain.
But let us keep things honest.
I cannot share with my heart uncovered.
Duplicity would not help but instead end in vain.
Running away and still, I will say.
Please live your life
Filled with harmony and delight.
While I run away tonight

SLUMBERING WAKE

Please do not ask why, but there is nowhere to go while I run and hide. I am lost and frozen, cold, buried deep and shallow—no way for me to reconcile my shattered memory. So, I settled for something lesser. I am dried out, empty, estranged from where I am and how I feel inside. It was so appealing that a day would warm a fire in the Arctic chill. My soul would quiver and be fleeting, taking my feet, and seeing if I could outpace all others. I was scant of emotion; my skipping beats and tripping ends caused my tongue to be bound. Do not flee from thought; I see nothing, not even that voice in the wind. It is all I can believe that this death is not my bed. My heart is not empty but filled with you instead.

Past Time to Dig

Grabbing a shovel, half a hole, will not make me sleep.
No song fills my ears.
The end of melodies, dying screams,
and scars from me tying my guts
There is no time for all my pain.
You cannot delve into my past and time without failing me.
You only feast centers on my insides
When will hope to become unburied?
Unravel the string, cut the cord, and birth anew my mind.
Traumas lay burdening.
But if only
I could find air and breathe it.
Just believe it.
Digging a hole to bury my memory
Climbing out of my consciousness

From the Grave to the Garden

Buried in the earth, a shattered stone.
Standing there, she is alone.
I walk, I cry, lose sight, I die.
Into the reach beyond all measure
Nothing for me or you but to be.
She says hello, but goodbye soon follows.
Today, the ash of sackcloth burnt.
Shed the poor man's rags and put on the garments of a king.
Crowns for the maiden and the pauper prince
Growing in the trees the apples, cherries, and peaches
A hello's last farewell, a sacred lotus
Blossom in your ways and work within your means
Are the grapes of the vineyard pressed in the morning?
Does the wine touch your lips to succor and bliss?

Waking in The Dark

Slumbering in the dead of night
As the terrors die, so does the dagger slip.
Into the lost beacons of the shadow
Sweat beat off a bloodied brow.
Waking up through the storms of solace
Will this delight of ours purge our iniquity?
Do the demons dance and trance and pass us by?
Can you slow the rhythm so that you can be with me in that moment?
She says the reason they are not what they seem to be.
The calloused memories, the lies deaf lips, and false cries of a remedy.
Will I see while I rise to wither and stand?
Bury me and fly left behind.
I sigh into the frigid night.
Wondering, pondering, and idling by
Does the slide slither and wind?
Can I breathe awake a pace and be less of a disgrace?
Can you see me and allow me to be a man to suit your love?

PREVAILING WINDS

Twice as hot as any Hellfire gate if once it was looked upon, then three times it was loosened. No matter of destiny forsaken a heresy. A burning sensation that can only be quenched by the thirst of the 10,000 maidens' stare. What was a part of me has flowered into fruition. A magnanimous empathy for those lost in the downward stair gleam. What was once and so again shall be a time, a sound, a rhyme of delight for the last sounding of the trumpets glistening. Again, arisen to the rising of the sunset, waiting for the morning and the dew. You and I are formed of destiny to behold a life fulfilled in fantasy. The lore of the land speaks, and the rider bore the scars of peace. Love is everlasting, and grace has never been foretold. The ecstasy of the divinity of truth is the path of this peace. No warfare is born without trickery and disdain. This rider, clothed in white, named free and true. Bear, all in sanctimony, a king no lower, no lesser. He is me, and I am him, the pauper prince and king.

Lift Me Up

Fly me high into the thunderous clouds.
There is no way for a cause without an apology from me.
As I say goodbye, tears and hills roll into the moon.
A sauntering kiss lasting but fleeting a moment retreating.
There is no way but to collapse under the pressure of my memories.
The retreat from my mind and lips pressed closed shut.
Amiss this happiness.
Like a jester without his cap
In pain for her and me
An absurdity of flattery gains me nothing.
Dry those eyelids and lift me from this bed.
As I lay as I die, can you complete me instead?

Like A Wildfire

Blazing eyes thorough in my memory
Nowhere to bide, nor ride, live free but buried inside.
Why would I not think I have lost all to gain?
When was I losing my demeanor and going insane?
If I could touch and be appeased, let loose, and see myself.
The garnering of truth sees the loss become known.
I once was apart but now have come to be.
In the presence of one so great and lovely as thee
Instead of making mistakes, I decry the me I see.
Take a new path across the way and see us in our pleasant dreams.
A spark in the grass shoots forth and ignites a price to be paid in me.
All for all, and nothing I can lose.
If I do not give in and realize that I have no state of mind

Standing Tall

Breaking up the weakened stance
Walking proud once more and gaining ground
I wake up to a new day, one filled with strength and peace.
The sanity of my sanctuary was restored.
My inner turmoil resolved.
I see without you in my mind, and there is no more need.
For my might is found within myself
Pressing forward as a man should
Gallant as the toughest knight
A boast of truth not replete
I see myself 10,000-fold stronger for the time we have shared.
But because of the need for luxury, I cannot afford it.
I have no time unless equality is restored.
Borrow the day, and the night should follow.
Bring the lost reality back to the present.
As I see a break in the day soon, does my afternoon follow.
With diligence and tactful ambition, I studiously vow.
To win, break free and no longer be bound.
No more chains nor longings
Lust nor throngs of added fill.
Only one I seek if even I would.
But only then if I am willing and if the worth is measured.
Not by my provision but by our binding prayers
Let loose the rays of heaven and shower me with praise.
The glory from God gives me the boldness of faith.

DESERT LANDS

I have come so far from the vast, dry, broken, and arid plains to find you. Where can I go that is not filled with poisonous snakes? Venomous tongues and bites from the seed are sown about in the gathering of sheep. Should we run, hide, look away, or give in? How do I climb this hill to overcome this burden of my sins? Should I be tepid, then my master will spew me out. So, I must climb, run, and carry with this in mind, with thoughts of you, too, in the arms of my Lord. Barren, though the land of my fortitude may be awkward, my past report. I seek to share my love with repentance so that tears of joy may shower these desert sands.

Grains of Sand

Shallow-struck dimly darkened, and caressed
This grave is the vesture of the poor man's king.
Cut the cord and denounce all inadequacy.
A volatile terrace of a battlefield solitude
Check the count and tally the fodder.
Pick up the candle and light the torch.
Cause for mayhem no more to be still.
With reckless abandon and no eyes cooled to chill
I see evil in the eyes of the world around.
Abroad of the serpent, the trickling of the sands
Eating dust and devouring all but I, and we
As prayers for all who may believe, pass lips not to deceive.
Also, for mercy in measure of greatest favor
Enable us to see our fantastic remedy.

Serpents Defeat

I am amongst the sheep, a wolf tamed by the shepherd's staff.

Idle goes the laying dog, waking up to see the slithering fiend.

To take the breath from the flock, making them into brood and snakes.

In the sands, the dust is eaten, the rod of comfort the Lord does speak,

"Fend off the foe who is the final woe!"

I pray that I may remain in God's Grace and take apart the wounded viper.

Give the Lord's word, partake, and be heard.

As death marches, so does the evil brigade.

A legion of many, the grief brought to light.

Should we all pray to remain and stay?

To comfort and praise, all will rise, and every knee shall bow.

Calling out Christ is Lord

Some shall rise forever and live.

Others shall descend in the dust and the wind.

The fires of pain, the driest of heats

Awaken the spirit within and cast away this valley of despair.

Parched in the Heat

I was looking for water, and you fed me dirt.
Shared with me a season for a time to be with no reason.
I saw a way out, but you did not listen.
I was hungry for more, and you fed me bars.
Lost in the way of no consequence in mind.
"Pay him no heed; he has no worth no deed."
Shouts from the masses from here to end from over there.
Silent pain that you fed me, calling me ungrateful.
As I am alone, they bury me. I die.
Will the Lord revive me?
Will I be worthy of love?
Does the prince go from pauper to bliss?

INTERLUDE

Traveling down the roads, we seem to depart on an awkward dream, a state of time with no way but to reconcile and pray. Walking down a second road appears to be a birthing pang where that morning dew falls away, the blistering heat of a beaten, sun-dried path. Do we stop to think or press onward to the desert sands? Storms ahead on the barren seas. Parting and retreating as I walk along, I thirst. Quench me, fill me, stir up my life with a trembling quake. When the earth shakes and the dust settles. I search and see no way without though I am standing tall and firm. Reckless, ruthless, and a brigand among the gathering of the fleece.

PART II

ALL IN TIME

Where are we going from this land to a new place? I sigh, let loose, pick myself up, and dry my eyes, a new man, no disguise. I look for the lady lost in my mind. Should I seek, run, and find? I am worthy a man and no less for loss in my life. I see a way, no time but a place to pray. Looking inward, I know the man standing tall once, twice, every, and all. Should I share with her my memories, the terrors and all? I should save grace, carry the burden, distill, and save face. In the highest of the mountain, I climb to the peak. The lowest of valleys cannot send me defeat. With the Lord as my guide, my banner, my father who carries me by his side.

There She Stands

Here, the maiden wakes in the dawning of the night
The hibiscus opens in the beautiful sunlight.
She is radiant in my presence, a measure of delight.
Never forsaken, my shadows are buried, dried up, never to tarry.
Our happiness is anew the vessels of the bells.
The clanging of the symbols announces their presence in the halls.
The darkness falls, and my eyes lift from their droop.
Seeing, believing, knowing, and loving
Hopes for us both, you, I, and we
Together, we share a life with tangled dreams.
No tattered souls sleeping all day.
But it is burgeoning with a flame that sparks a new wave.
I see the road on which she stands.
Down the way, my hope leads down the hall.
Reminiscent in waves, it is you I crave.
To see it speak it.
Could you look at me and embrace me?

Boldness of the Prince

The peace of mind I gather from her is cooling.
This prince, not a fiend, slips down on bended knee.
A proposition the aspirations of love for the Orchid Queen
The maiden's delight in the cunning prince would derive.
Where two or more are gathered, a hundred more applaud the scene.
Being a blessed ceremony, the coming glory for the king
Who once was lowly, lonely, and lost.
But now is found, familiar, and faithful.
Blessed be the peacemakers who come bearing the truth.
Ride on the winds in the coming of the dark.
Dawn in the night, the thoroughfares suddenly delightful
Pressing in for the wedded kiss
No more a pauper or prince but a king of married virtue to both wife and land
For one of sudden courage to take a fair lass by the hand
The last calling of a trumpet was the beginning of a new era.
A man, a woman, one peace in harmony and of accord

Who am I?

What dreams do we appease when we tire and rest our weary heads?
Do we seek the best or bury our withered stems?
Will I love her like no other or break my mind in twain?
Father, I plead on this broken, bent knee that I can fulfill in duty and triumph to all satisfaction and glory.
No one knows me like I would hope, but instead, they judge me by my misdeeds.
I was shattered, battered, torn, and scattered, born in light shadows.
Create a new song for me, a melody to match a harmonious heart.
Thrilling, bone-chilling, well-crafted, and worn.
A love wore on the seats of royal duality.
What once was low but lifted high.
Both uplifting and sublime end-to-break
To bring together in one accord one body, one mind, one way, one truth, one life

THE BREAKING WIND

The whirling, twirling flag rolls, unfurling the colors of peace. As we ride along this valley in line with God's creation, I admire the beauty he created in femininity—a gorgeous woman of distinction more than all with an aroma finer than sweet alyssum. A gaze into the blazing fire warming and cooling as my heart feints, not discontent nor malcontent but extravagance brimming with delight. A heartfelt prayer, a hallelujah to the Lord God, all praise. Where was this tranquility born in admiration soul for matching soul? Do we see all in love and shout hosanna to the God above? Mighty Father, bless us together as we go down our path grace and honor bound. Glory be to you and me through him as we ride into the sun's setting.

Soaring Eagles

Birds of prey in flight to the mountainous peak
Rising in the darkness of the night by the fire of flame and passion, bright
To see one another, each with an end to meet in the sleek middling of the ground and terrace.
Reminisce together in unity, all wings grounded and lifted above, symbolizing embrace.
Sweet and tender, which hugging motion carries them everywhere, holding them like no other.
Two of one mind and matching accord bring us together and feast upon our fate.
Of circumstances that kept them apart, none could last in the wake.
For she and I are lovely together, two birds without feathers.
The world wakes, stirs, lays like baked clay, and is molded.
The potter weaves and makes our bed together in the pleasant valley.
Down from the mountain into the sparkling streams below
Where eagles match doves, and we all dance for love.
No pass at the finer lass or this eagle will pass by with claws and snatch.
A heart flutters all eyes and shudders, quickening in the darkness of the dawn.

Warmer Waters

The coolness of May is tempered by the warmest springs.
I was baking in the water, wading, cascading, calm, and calling out.
We see each other passing by, and we stop and stay as we long to do.
Will we meet in the middle of the liquid pool?
Where we stop, look, and revere without fear, tear, or jaded sneer.
Shallow ends where the rivers bend, the spring storms cannot touch.
She calls me, "Come close so we can have each other and hold."
I am eager to complete the intervention that meets the ends that beat.
The hearts are entwined with spirituality in mind.
Caressing souls, each meeting is a match that makes the world envious.
In embrace, they chase, stir up, run away, and save face.
Leaving the world behind for a better place

Home and Hearth

The charcoal ash and sudden winds spying eyes and lovely wings.
Pressed together, the amber of ambiguity in expressing our passion.
Both in unison, adventurous and bold, a cavern no longer a king with my hold
The dawn of light glistening off the Queen of my heart
She is the most pleasing in the demeanor of rare beauty as if a vice with no venom but spice.
Her face leaves me nestled in the comfort of her tacit embrace.
Gliding effortlessly and purely out of the fountains of fire
Refined, more elegant than gold and silver, even more pure.
Rushing winds never were so complete until I gazed at how she moved from her head to her feet.
The last time I saw it, I was not lost but replete.
Filled with honeysuckle and dewdrop, the mountain, the valley, oh dear lady of mine
You are so delicate, and I will love you until the end of time.

PASSING THE IDLE TIME

Down the way, I see that I say stop by for you someday. As I pass by, I look for her bounty, and the dirt hits my face. I dig my grave, which is a man's final rest—a whole fit for all regret and due shame. I bury my burdens, squalor, misdeeds, and my shame. There is no pride in my tears. Will you all still accept me? Will the world pass me by? Does the Glory of God lift the sunken demeanor of my face? The hours pass, and I can only see my demise. Withered, blood-stained, and gathered to die. So, to the Father, I pray, dear Lord, keep at bay all the trappings of prison and let the sun stay to rise.

Picking up the Pieces

Drowning in the seas of my past
Looking abroad for the bringing of the axe
Slamming down the gavel, it reported my departure.
Airing out my last breath in the shadows of the serpent tide
Break me apart and show me who I am.
Send from here to the shadowed lands.
I will survive with God as a guide.
The painstaking truth is the breath of life.
That sets boats to sail upon the heavenly seas.
From here to there and through all trial and storm
Stop upon the bend that meets each end.
Breaking my mind
Loosening the axe and severing the serpent from the vine

Without Him

You weep wherefore you are weary.
Bleed tears; therefore, you were humble.
The boundless sky ripped with ground shaking.
Without the sacrifice of the True King
There would be no I nor you nor we
We all would be in the trappings of a mortal guise.
Sent without the pure love of God.
For without a savior, how could we also live?
When we see ourselves in love with one another
Do we bleed for each other as well?
Do we posit our innermost feelings?
Or do we do as we need and pray for guidance instead?

Waking up to Her

Opening the grave, she looks into my eyes.
Lifting the lids without a flinching or a cry
Waking up, my heart beats and stirs one more time.
My breathing realigns, and I stand to an embrace.
Oh Lord my God, thank you for her, my lovely bride.
The day I died to self, and I rose by her side.
We joined together, and I pledged to coincide.
The passing of the time waiting for my bride
As I hunger as I thirst by the side of each rode
Standing on the mountain, with no regret left for the bold
Hear me, my father, as I slumber and wake.
Break free the rope and cut all ties.
Loosen the bonds and fill me with life.

DARLING IN THE EVENING

A fever of the heart is a definition of love and peace everlasting. Does the hummingbird flutter and fly? Does the dew draw nearer? Can I open, embrace, and overcome all lasting fear? It is a time to dance, a time to sing. At times, to pass away fears. Ease into movements, glide, slide, and live like no other moment. Hand to hand, a rousing applause as we traverse the way to the kingdom and the many thrones. Heaven above you are a darling in the evening. There is no way without our way to begin. There is only the blessing of the Father, God, and The King, Eternal. Life Everlasting Prince of Peace, one olive branch descending. The ripened vine his Eternal Grace. The Glory of God is mighty within. Make me a knight for love and everlasting life.

In Your Greatest Measure

The greatest treasure of my innermost desires
Is it to be in equanimity with your soul?
The tallest trees are not more spacious than the depths of my love for you.
Seeing you go by the olive tree; I bask in your presence.
You are more abundant than Gilead in balm and fragrance.
The pomegranate does not touch the taste of your kiss.
You are sweeter than honey and finer than silk.
Your hair is like strands of wisteria.
In the air, you walk, and in you, I breathe.

The Grace that Breaks

Calling down the lightning, the thunders roar in mighty winds.
Splattering, maddening, scattering the potter bakes the clay.
Earth to shake and to raise the son of the prince.
Does the cradle rock and the stairway sway?
Ladders to doorways and divine interpretation sought.
Shake the foundation and shatter the mold.
Breaking all chains and bearing all scars
From here to there is forbearance appreciated in measure
Applied in time, the ties that bind match eye for tooth and nail, implied.
God's true glory and Grace, unmatched, sends the pauper to his knees.
Bow down the prince on the broken, wounded knee.
The tide flows no way to know the peace that makes all virtue.
This day is a time to say.
To reconnect, dwell a while, and cohabitate in mind.
All intellect and duality aside, let us play the pauper's lute.
The bard with many tales, the songs with many devices
Pluck the strings and accord a fair truth.
For melody is a harmony when contracted for meshing heart
When soul and spirit revive the body
We will all be whole.

Waiting for You

When there is no time to spare, I would rather live in the presence of your mind.
I would find one thinking only of you and bliss when there is no reason.
There is no lasting memory without the changing of the seasons.
No greater burden than to bear it without a woman as fine as you.
Peace is only found in love when the Lord deems it so
We can only find one another with the blessings of the truth.
So, we stop and search for we are lonely and separated.
Will we find each other on the other side of the mist and vapor?
Will you be waiting for me to be whole again?
As I am for you to be blessed in unison

SOLDIER OF FORTUNE

Sometimes, battles are reserved for those who can oversee most—through trust in God and his mightiness brought to boast. Some are brave soldiers of war, some struggle in the clouds above, and many still battle on the plains of spirituality. Principalities and warrior spirits, colliding and cascading, the stars that fall and those that come in the clouds. Heaven's Warriors battling with all presence of mind. Some may know, and others may see who I am and what we are one day. Galloping by a troubadour, priest, and I suddenly said, "One for God, all for one, and many triumphs in victory." So, the story continues, and I awaken not from a slumber or sleep but from a battle eternal through the heavenly feats.

On the Plains of Heaven

In paradise, God reigns eternal through his mightiness and virtue, bold
While Lucifer condemns and derides us for our very souls
Should we pray for mercy to Christ the Prince of Peace
The King of kings makes us the warriors that we are.
So, we can fight for good and win the day.
For the devil cannot devour what he cannot slay
He may not touch the truth of our spirits and cannot rid us of salvation.
For God is the one true judge, the leader of all nations.
With rod and staff, the leader at mass derides and ends all the cries.
The healing from temptation

Fighting the Past

From youth, the demons speak and run around the mountainous peak.
Traipsing in to cause all sin and divide the mind, the battle begins.
The devil speaks to temptations bleak and instigates the feud.
With all to imbue, it all ensues, never knowing a cause for the ends and the means.
There is no reason to justify the intensified combat.
The screeching, scratching, back against the wall timeless nerve-racking
We find the pauper as he struggles to make his way.
With God in mind, he prays daily to make him a humble man.
But if the devil had his way to prison, he would stay from here until the end.
Freed in Christ is the triumphant cry of the battle against all evil
Shall we wait, or should we run the mighty race?
From here to there, the end and beginning of all grace foretold.

COME LORD JESUS COME

When will it be the sights, the sounds, the trumpets blast? Will I cry tears like rain as the sky mourns the passing of the day? Should the sights, the sounds, the brothers, and sisters be troubled by the richness of cowardly men? Trouble not from the cowards' gleam. The God above triumphs from Jerusalem thereof, instead of men who are froth, withered, and boiled with wroth, for when heaven comes and the sighting of the Son of God and man, his strong hand delivers. An end to tribulation for God almighty reigns forever in Grace. In his truths, do we adhere to the commands given by the Father? So, to all faithful, we shall cry, Come, Lord Jesus, Come.

Bless Us, O Lord

We beg of you, O God, we plead!
Restore our sanity in earnestness and kindness.
Our bodies are your temple.
No other sacrifice do we need.
You are the fulfilling Lamb, the breath of all that breathes.
Humble us and enlighten us on the cause of all that bleed.
For this prince who, for his love, seeks only your approval.
But if you should ordain and see me fit, it is the orchid that which I will seek.
The discourse of harmony is an exposition of our souls.
Seeking not the world's ambitions, replacing them with God's good gift of Grace

Sanctify Our Spirits

In God's Holy sight by the lighting in the day
Send the towers to their knees, the mighty to their downfall.
The arbor of tranquility, a fleeting sightless austerity
The methods of peace abound in more than a memory.
Take the tide, gather the nets, and gather us in with posterity.
Our spirits gather, waiting for a candle to light our wick.
From passing by to transformations of deliverance
In your honor, we seek the diligence of our king.
The God of all and all to praise
Dwell in us, amongst, and pass not between
There is no way for us to shirk our responsibility.
Or for us to decide with a compass of glass
Even I, the pauper, seek the paved roads of the King of Kings

Justify Our Steps

The Judge of Peace condemns not our walk.
Trusting in him presents us with a new way to talk.
Giving into the precepts of a principled man
The Son of God, the God of Man
Enlightens us lest we err.
Knowledge brought forth to captivate our souls.
Trappings of the world disguised, boastful, riddled with lies.
We beg and plead, seek, pray, and are weak.
Looking for the hope of bringing us to our knees
Our way, our truth, our paths set straight.
For his are sharper than any sword and finer than any silk
By wound, we are duller and more woolen.
Deliver and heal, brighten with serenity.
The break of day light the dawning of the night

INTERLUDE

Where is the light in the morning, the break of day? Did I squander my love for frivolity and vice? Did I thrice more and again? I am the plundered, the vagabond, this fugitive of sanctimony. The tapping of the heart, the beating of the mind. Should I face, embrace, and wonder what may take place? With eyes in mind and destiny entwined, it is today that I find I should be inclined to pass by. Without apprehension and admonition, a certain lack of determination, I am subtly slyly asking to walk on. Then is sought the heartful peace, a fluttering vexation of inward bliss—a twitch of the wrists and a parting of the ways. Should I seek to stop and stay? Run away or by turmoil set the break the switch in the windowpane? On this day, I will leave my sanity behind, run free, and outlast my present thoughts.

SEEKING THE LOST WAY

The lips lie those shining eyes peaking from around a brook. When I seek in you a mystery, will I delve into the depths of eternity? There is now that I shall stop this minute and behold each second as the last one drips and falls into the most profound chasm. Bloodshot eyes from hours of strain. A part of me wishes for the tears to fall, and another sees the dreams as they beckon and call. The nights accord the pack of all the roots of the fall do not trouble as I set apart instead. Change my mind, and I will see a way to you the sprouting limbs of a fruitful tree. Life-giving and sustaining in your ways, I stop and ponder the route I was on before the madness fled my mind. Replace it with serenity, not entangled with a lonesome draw. Pass by day and into the gloves at night, stuck with the shadows lingering nearby. I walk down a beaten path. I am dogged and ragged, torn apart and surrendered. I plead, I seek, I stop speaking. Where do I go to tally the days when I am lost in the cave? Does this light peer in, or will I wither in my sin? Is there a hand to hold or I to never know, lost, broken, beaten, and sold? A price not paid for a vice not taken near or far cast astray and scared from here below to the valley and beyond.

Whether Near or Far

The truth, the hope, the beckoned call
One love in mind searching, lurking, and retreating into my soul.
The cairn slips, and the rocks slide in a ruthless tumult
Eager means meager dreams of sunset and sunshine in serenity
Harmony lost a quaint view oppressed with pleasure in my distress.
When juxtaposed with a tear for a measure of barley?
Wheat is refined, but what a time I should see, lest it be the dreary or the highlands.
The plains, the mains, or seeing down the road.
My dearest friend, the one whom I most thought I would fancy.
For the stars that shine, the moon outlasts sight for loss, something to consider.
When will I stop this bleeding from a bandaged wound?
Will I plead to thee indeed and mend the heart again?

Death's Shadow

Israel O' Israel, where did we depart?
Does the moon hide where the leper sleeps?
Do fountains spring from the daggers of the night lest the sparrows keep?
In this valley, this shadow of death lays deceit
The ember burns the mountainous peaks.
Lest we beckon, the fiery tempest speaks.
Of crags, slag, and mortar, barren left bleak
Do we find at all the ageless diamonds meek?
Is there a standing left among the desert seas?
A way to lay upon the water crest.
In the rivers of solace, is there a way to behold?
The last the first, the desert hold
Shakes, quakes, and snakes of dancing weather breaks
Looming where the lions meet
The ox, the mule, and the wolf retreat
Passing guards, the sulfur breaks
Retreat, the feat, never the sheep.
This lamb, I am the desert sands.
Standing on the valley's cliff
No fear, no tear, never hear, never too barren or deep.
Rise arose, foretold, and behold.
Keys to death of Hellfire's defeat
Coming, come, arise to set aside.
Apart from the bridegroom, does he sleep?
The weathered eyes coincide with a matching loom for threaded needle spurred.

Onward they go a death they do not know a time, or time, or half or more.

Find the tree the branch in thee.

Forsake, not courage. Grant the wisdom to speak.

Idle mind for a time to bind rapped inside and buried alive.

Crooked shears for weathered gear bandaged in graves worried for servant's sake.

Running the race at the pace of his Grace, no sake for sanity.

Run in the grass, the rain, the wind, the bleary main.

Cross the crown withered, and brown became a King of snow frost peak.

Lightning peals and rainbows grain

The sight to see between you and me, I love for thee to open and breathe.

Partake for sake, and see and wake up. Open those eyes, both miry and tired.

I see the dew that grew tethered and through once, twice, thrice, bold, and new.

I was born again, woken to wake, and ferried to fate.

All entwined to those that pry lay close the spry or else laid to die.

Forsworn to deed in action to impart by the blade of flame to guard and impart.

It is selected to select pardoned to reply and only to go within.

Have faith, and behold, all will be told.

The bridegroom meets the bride.

Fires of Virtue

By Cherubim's blade, flames, and staves
Fighting fast and embers
The flash of light falling from stars was once called mighty.
Great and bold withered-in folds
A war in heaven loosed, and enemies made.
A shout, a blast, a tyrannical gasp seizing humanity's minds.
Snares and poisonous pitfalls weathered as lightning storms.
Peace ensues, a rainbow looms, and the dawning of the time.
As the cradle rocks, the bow of the ship dips, slides, and hits the tides.
Upward to peer and seem sincere while holding on to life.
He paid for tithe, then bought the pile.
A time for war, a time for peace
A time to marry, seek love, and boast in the Lord.
As the sparrow flies, so does the worm crawl.
Do we seek for the garden with bushels and all?
Will all the grain a plight of might call us to our knees?
Does the boulder sink, or do the mighty mountains move?
Raining in the day, the shadows loom, and the darkness meets our eyes.
Blind by the eve of the break of fall to the day of winter delight
Should I pay into the thunderous clouds of billowed moats?
Virtues of destiny to be tried in serenity
The Shining Star was born on the day the Lord was made.
Salvation of Grace abounding in the waves, true peace for a meal without fleece
The time at the end is a way to bend the showing of the guard.

Arise the one, the many, the few, the only, the true
By creed indeed, I stop to see the supper of the lamb.

WORDS OF WISDOM

The Wise Man

A wise man stores his treasures in heaven.
Chief amongst them are the people whom God adores.
Those of all nations, tribes, and tongues
God blesses those who bless others.
A prophet who is wise seeks God first
God's word is what passes from his lips.
He carries it from here to where it is called.
God executes his judgment by his word.
In this judgment, the wise man seeks to meditate.
He uses it as a breath of his life.

The Ruler

The ruling man who covets his possessions tastes poison in his cup
Favors of speech and posturing before the God above
He does not see like the blind man who reckons with his soul.
There is no thread to weave nor burden borne.
In his hastened lore, he spreads his wares within
Age-old sin and passing grace no robes to clothe him now.
He sees as he pleases, passing the time with the debt he gambles.

The Foolish Man

A foolish man seeks gains in himself.
He ambles about in poverty of speech.
Flattery of wit that is pervasive and perverse.
He is a man who seeks gratuities for favors.
One of deception and deceit
He is clouded in his mind and judges with a dishonest tongue.
Anger is his justice, and dissolution is his drink.
His cup is filled with the wine of wrath.
He drinks in the wine and splendor of the kings of men.

The Sightless Beggar

The man who cannot see still feels.
Does not the man who sees still embrace?
Without sight, a man can remain reliant on God.
His faith is in God's mercy.
Mercy that heals the pains that ail
Is his faith found in sight?
Or visions of the kingdom of God
Where we find in him is his grace, mercy, and peace.
The blinded man can see within.

AUTHOR'S THOUGHTS

Justification

Salvation—Salvation is a gift of God's Grace. You can reject a gift. A gift can be disgracefully returned. Or a gift that can be accepted through perseverance and good faith.

Free Will—Assuming our state of being, if there is no free will, there will be no sin or righteousness. The fact that there is both constitutes free will. Predestination does not mean that we are chosen in the sense that we are forced or given a choice but rather spurred on by the spirit. The deciding factor is personal and found in grace and perseverance. Perseverance is not of works but faith. Faith will set you free, not works. Works are deeds done as an act of God of proof of faith and belief.

Baptism—We are commanded to be baptized as a part of belief. Not because we believe but instead as an act of obedience to God's commands. The heart of baptism is that we seek in faith and belief to achieve the fullest measure of the Grace that God seeks to impart upon us. As Christ was baptized, so should we follow in his ways.

Repentance—Turning from sin requires faith and belief in Grace. Grace enables repentance through his righteousness. The Holy Spirit's growth can overcome all manners of spiritual warfare. Though we may sin, we must remember that through faith and belief, we overcome not through our deeds but through God's words and strength. To all who seek, he shall find; to all who lend an ear, let them hear.

Righteousness—Righteousness is imparted by faith and belief through the Holy Spirit and Grace. We believe in Jesus Christ as our example and our higher power.

Justification—We are justified through the Righteousness and Holiness of Christ Jesus. Through His shed blood on the Cross. We are redeemed from the wages of sin and death and reborn in Christ. As such, we are deemed worthy of the kingdom of heaven. Not by our admission but through the Gift of salvation.

Final Thought—While we may all know ourselves to be sinners as we continue in such. I would consider that we all should share the light as we are led and be good soldiers for Christ.

JOHN 3:1-21 (KJV)

¹There was a man of the Pharisees, named Nicodemus, a ruler of the Jews:

² The same came to Jesus by night, and said unto him, Rabbi, we know that thou art a teacher come from God: for no man can do these miracles that thou doest, except God be with him.

³ Jesus answered and said unto him, Verily, verily, I say unto thee, Except a man be born again, he cannot see the kingdom of God.

⁴ Nicodemus saith unto him, How can a man be born when he is old? Can he enter the second time into his mother's womb, and be born?

⁵ Jesus answered, Verily, verily, I say unto thee, Except a man be born of water and of the Spirit, he cannot enter into the kingdom of God.

⁶ That which is born of the flesh is flesh; and that which is born of the Spirit is spirit.

⁷ Marvel not that I said unto thee, Ye must be born again.

⁸ The wind bloweth where it listeth, and thou hearest the sound thereof, but canst not tell whence it cometh, and whither it goeth: so is every one that is born of the Spirit.

⁹ Nicodemus answered and said unto him, How can these things be?

¹⁰ Jesus answered and said unto him, Art thou a master of Israel, and knowest not these things?

¹¹ Verily, verily, I say unto thee, We speak that we do know, and testify that we have seen; and ye receive not our witness.

¹² If I have told you earthly things, and ye believe not, how shall ye believe, if I tell you of heavenly things?

¹³ And no man hath ascended up to heaven, but he that came down from heaven, even the Son of man which is in heaven.

¹⁴ And as Moses lifted up the serpent in the wilderness, even so must the Son of man be lifted up:

¹⁵ That whosoever believeth in him should not perish, but have eternal life.

¹⁶ For God so loved the world, that he gave his only begotten Son, that whosoever believeth in him should not perish, but have everlasting life.

¹⁷ For God sent not his Son into the world to condemn the world; but that the world through him might be saved.

¹⁸ He that believeth on him is not condemned: but he that believeth not is condemned already, because he hath not believed in the name of the only begotten Son of God.

¹⁹ And this is the condemnation, that light is come into the world, and men loved darkness rather than light, because their deeds were evil.

²⁰ For every one that doeth evil hateth the light, neither cometh to the light, lest his deeds should be reproved.

²¹ But he that doeth truth cometh to the light, that his deeds may be made manifest, that they are wrought in God.

www.ingramcontent.com/pod-product-compliance
Lightning Source LLC
Chambersburg PA
CBHW072023060426
42449CB00034B/2072